Scary Creatures
PINNIPEDS

Written by
John Malam

Created and designed
by David Salariya

Franklin Watts®
An Imprint of Scholastic Inc.
NEW YORK • TORONTO • LONDON • AUCKLAND • SYDNEY
MEXICO CITY • NEW DELHI • HONG KONG
DANBURY, CONNECTICUT

Author:

John Malam studied ancient history and archeology at the University of Birmingham, England. He then worked as an archeologist at the Ironbridge Gorge Museum in Shropshire. He is now an author specializing in nonfiction books for children on a wide range of subjects. He lives in Cheshire, England, with his wife and their two young children. Website: www.johnmalam.co.uk

Artists:

Janet Baker and Julian Baker
  (JB Illustrations)
Robert Morton
Carolyn Franklin
Mark Bergin

Series Creator:

David Salariya was born in Dundee, Scotland. In 1989 he established The Salariya Book Company. He has illustrated a wide range of books and has created many new series for publishers in the UK and overseas. He lives in Brighton, England, with his wife, illustrator Shirley Willis, and their son.

Editor: Tanya Kant

Editorial Assistant:
Rob Walker

Picture Research:
Mark Bergin, Carolyn Franklin

Photo Credits:

Dreamstime: 11, 15, 25, 29
Fotolia: 19, 24
iStockphoto: 9, 12, 16, 17, 18, 20–21, 22, 23, 26, 28

Trained sea lion

Created, designed, and produced by
The Salariya Book Company Ltd
25 Marlborough Place, Brighton BN1 1UB

A CIP catalog record for this title is available from the Library of Congress.

ISBN-13: 978-0-531-21672-9 (Lib. Bdg.)
978-0-531-21043-7 (Pbk.)
ISBN-10: 0-531-21672-1 (Lib. Bdg.)
0-531-21043-X (Pbk.)

Published in 2010 in the United States by
Franklin Watts
An Imprint of Scholastic Inc.
557 Broadway
New York, NY 10012

Printed in China

PAPER FROM
SUSTAINABLE
FORESTS

Contents

Walrus

What Are Pinnipeds?

Pinnipeds are **mammals** that live in the sea, in freshwater, and on land and ice. They live in the icy Arctic and Antarctic oceans, and in warmer waters around the world. *Pinniped* means "fin-footed," which gives us a clue about how these animals move. When they are on land or ice, they use their fins, or flippers, to move around.

There are 33 different **species** of pinnipeds. These species are grouped into three families: **phocids** (true seals), **otariids** (sea lions and fur seals), and **odobenids** (walruses).

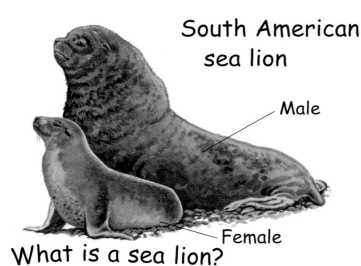

South American sea lion

Male

Female

Leopard seal

What is a sea lion?

A sea lion is a pinniped known as an otariid. Fur seals are also otariids. Otariids are called eared seals because they have tiny ear flaps on the outside of their bodies. Their hind (back) flippers are hairless. An otariid can turn these flippers forward and walk on them like feet.

What is a seal?

A seal is a pinniped known as a phocid. A phocid is also called a true seal or earless seal. It does not have ear flaps on the outside of its body. Instead, it has tiny ear holes. Its hind flippers are furry and cannot be folded underneath its body to be used as feet.

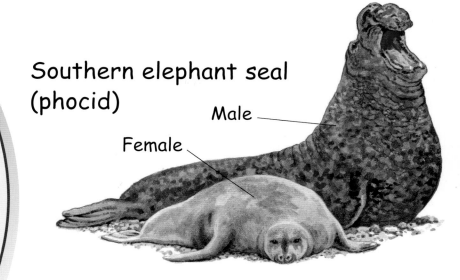
Southern elephant seal (phocid)

Male

Female

Northern fur seal (otariid)

Male

Female

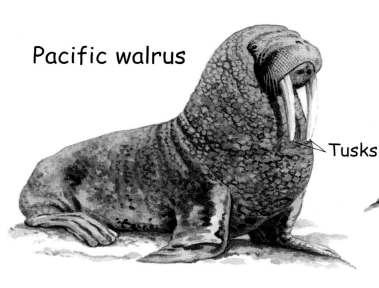

Pacific walrus

Tusks

What is a walrus?

A walrus is a pinniped known as an odobenid. Like a phocid, an odobenid has no ear flaps. Like an otariid, it can use its hind flippers as feet when it is on land. Its upper **canine teeth** have developed into two long tusks.

How big are pinnipeds?

Pinnipeds vary in size, depending on the species. The smallest pinniped is the Baikal seal, found only in Lake Baikal, Russia. It grows to about 4.6 feet (1.4 m) long. The longest pinniped is the southern elephant seal, which grows to 16 feet (5 m). The heaviest pinniped is also the southern elephant seal, which weighs up to 4.5 tons.

How Does a Pinniped Swim?

Pinnipeds have smooth, rounded bodies that move quickly through water. Pinnipeds can swim fast for short distances, but most of the time they swim at a steady cruising speed.

X-Ray Vision

Hold the next page up to the light to see what's inside a leopard seal.

See what's inside

Seals and walruses swim by moving their hind flippers from side to side. They use their front flippers for steering. Sea lions, however, swim with their front flippers and steer with their hind flippers.

Hind flippers

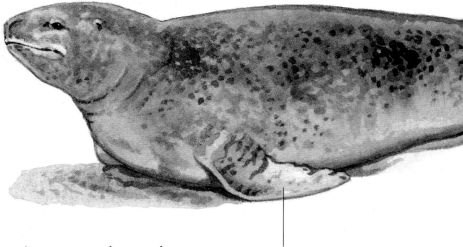

Leopard seal

Front flippers

Pinnipeds get their round shape from the thick layer of fat underneath their skin. This **blubber** keeps them warm and allows them to live in cold places.

6

Leopard seal

Smooth, rounded body

Thick, short fur

Hind flipper

Short, thick neck

Front flipper

Short whiskers

Chinstrap penguin

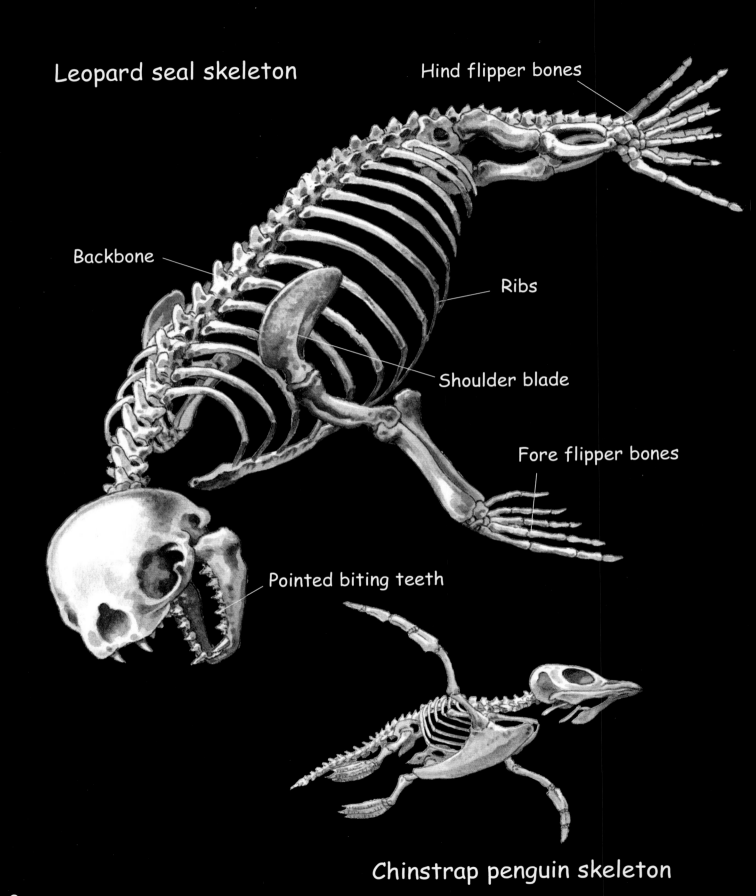

Leopard seal skeleton

Hind flipper bones

Backbone

Ribs

Shoulder blade

Fore flipper bones

Pointed biting teeth

Chinstrap penguin skeleton

8

What's Inside a Pinniped?

All pinnipeds have large skulls and flexible skeletons. Seals and sea lions have pointed teeth that can catch and hold onto slippery **prey** such as fish and squid. Walruses have front teeth that have grown into tusks.

Why do walruses have tusks?

Walruses use their tusks to pull themselves out of the water and onto the ice. During their breeding season, male walruses display their tusks to attract females or defend a mating territory from other males. Males' tusks are longer and heavier than those of females.

Why do pinnipeds swallow stones?

Gastroliths

Many pinnipeds swallow small stones. These stones, known as **gastroliths**, stay in their stomachs. Scientists think these stones might grind up food, making it easier to digest. Or the stones may help pinnipeds keep their balance underwater.

Adult walruses displaying their tusks to each other

What Do Pinnipeds Eat?

Pinnipeds are **carnivores** (meat-eaters). They eat mainly small sea animals, especially fish, shrimp, **krill**, octopus, and squid. Leopard seals eat larger animals such as penguins and other pinnipeds. Walruses prefer to eat animals that live on the seabed, such as clams, crabs, and sea cucumbers.

Leopard seals catch penguins either by chasing them underwater or by breaking through thin ice and snatching them from below. The seal tosses the penguin around, beating it against the water until it is dead and its skin comes off. Then the seal eats the body. It doesn't eat the feathers, skin, feet, or beak.

How does a walrus eat a clam?

First, the walrus finds the clam by stirring up mud on the seabed, either with its front flippers or by squirting water out of its mouth. Then it sucks the clam from its shell or blasts it out with a jet of water. A walrus can find and eat six clams a minute!

Pinniped prey

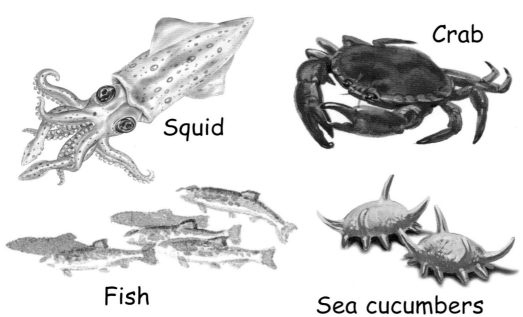

Squid

Crab

Fish

Sea cucumbers

Adélie penguin

Krill

Did You Know?

In 1967, four leopard seals killed 15,000 penguins on Ross Island, Antarctica, in 15 weeks. One seal ate six penguins in 70 minutes.

This sea lion has just caught a fish.

The sea lion eats the fish's body but leaves the head and tail.

11

How Deep Can Pinnipeds Dive?

Pinnipeds can dive to great depths and can stay underwater for a long time. Elephant seals dive the deepest, down to 4,100 feet (1,250 m). Walruses are shallow divers that rarely go deeper than 260 feet (80 m).

How long can a pinniped hold its breath?

A walrus can hold its breath for about ten minutes and a sea lion for about 20 minutes. A Weddell seal can stay submerged for 70 minutes. A southern elephant seal can stay underwater for two hours before returning to the surface for air.

X-Ray Vision

Hold the next page up to the light to see what's about to grab a seal.

See what happens

A walrus swimming underwater

Young elephant seal

Female elephant seal

Male elephant seal

13

Killer whale

Young seal

Who Preys on Pinnipeds?

Pinnipeds have many **predators**. On land and ice, pinnipeds are attacked for their meat by polar bears, wolves, eagles, pumas, and brown hyenas. Humans also hunt them for their fur, blubber, and meat. At sea, pinnipeds are hunted by sharks and killer whales. Pinnipeds also attack and eat other pinnipeds.

Out at sea, killer whales herd seals together and swim through the group to grab individuals. They also snatch seals from the shore, almost **beaching** themselves as they lunge at the surprised seals.

Did You Know?

Polar bears have been seen throwing chunks of ice at walruses and seals, perhaps to stun them before moving in for the kill.

In the Arctic, polar bears hunt seals, especially ringed seals.

What Is the Life Cycle of a Pinniped?

Pinniped mothers carry their babies inside them for about 11 months. Babies, called **pups**, are born on land or ice. Pups feed on their mother's fat-rich milk and quickly gain weight. After they are **weaned**, the pups leave their mothers. The pups will start their own families when they are about four years old.

Pinnipeds live for about 15 to 25 years. Female pinnipeds (called **cows**) live longer than males (called **bulls**). It's thought that pinnipeds live longer in the wild than in zoos.

Galápagos sea lion mother feeding her pup with milk

16

A large **colony** of Cape fur seals in Namibia, southern Africa

Some pinnipeds, such as Ross seals, Baikal seals, and crabeater seals, are solitary animals—they live on their own. Others, such as elephant seals, sea lions, and walruses, live in groups. During their breeding seasons, some seals come ashore in large numbers to form **rookeries**—colonies where pinnipeds breed and raise their young together.

Why Do Pinnipeds Shed Their Fur?

Seals and sea lions have thick fur that helps to keep them warm. Every so often, pinnipeds shed their old fur, and new fur grows in its place. This process is called **molting**. Most pinnipeds molt every year, which keeps their coats healthy. They stay out of the cold water until their new fur has grown.

Did You Know?

It takes a fur seal up to three years to shed its thick coat of fur. It keeps some old fur for warmth while its new fur grows. There are nearly 300,000 hairs in every square inch of its fur!

Adult male

Young seal

Newborn pup

This is a family of elephant seals. Pups are born with black fur. They shed this fur after they are weaned.

Elephant seal shedding its old fur

Some pinnipeds, such as elephant seals, shed their fur quickly and in patches. They find a safe place to come ashore, called a **haul-out**, and then shed all their fur in about one month. This is called a "catastrophic" molt because it happens suddenly and dramatically. It sounds painful, but it's not.

A pup's first coat of fur, called **lanugo**, is made of soft, delicate hair. Harbor seals shed their lanugo while they are inside their mothers. They are born with a warm adult coat. Elephant seals are born with black lanugo, which is shed for a coat of silvery-gray adult fur.

How Far Do Pinnipeds Travel?

Some pinnipeds—such as northern fur seals, harp seals, and walruses—**migrate**. This means that they swim long distances every year to and from their breeding grounds and feeding grounds. Northern elephant seals make the longest journeys. Each year they swim from breeding grounds in Mexico and California to feeding grounds in the northern Pacific Ocean and Alaska, and back again.

Did You Know?

Male and female northern elephant seals have separate feeding grounds. Scientists are not sure why. Every year, males swim about 13,000 miles (21,000 km) and females swim 11,000 miles (18,000 km).

Migratory pinnipeds return to the same breeding and feeding grounds year after year. How they find their way is a mystery. They seem to have a built-in "compass" that points the way. But water and wind currents, and the taste and temperature of the sea probably guide them, too.

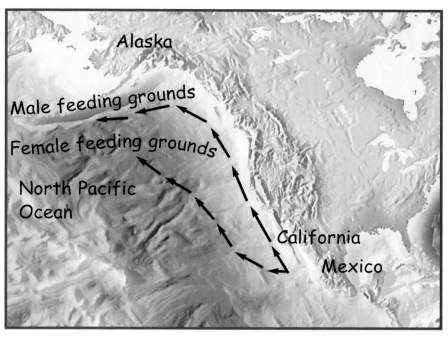

Migration route of northern elephant seals

Do all pinnipeds migrate?

Not all pinnipeds are migratory. Harbor seals, leopard seals, gray seals, and many sea lion species spend all their lives within the same area.

Northern elephant seals spend most of their lives at sea.

Why Do Pinnipeds Sing?

Pinnipeds make many different sounds, both under the water and on land. During the breeding season, male pinnipeds will make threat calls, telling others to stay away. Pinnipeds make calls to warn each other when predators are near. Weddell seals and walruses make various grunts, whines, yelps, chirps, whistles, and barks. Sometimes these noises sound a little like singing.

Did You Know?

A male elephant seal's nose looks like a short trunk, which is how it got its name. In the breeding season the male forces air through its nose, making noises to keep other males away.

A male walrus can sing for two or three minutes at a time. It has a range of deep notes and high whistles. It also makes clicks with its teeth and may slap its throat pouch with its flippers to make loud noises.

Each colony of northern elephant seals has its own **dialect**, or range of sounds.

A California sea lion barking

Are Pinnipeds in Danger?

Because of **global warming**, some pinnipeds, such as those in the Arctic and Antarctic, are in danger. The temperature of some oceans is increasing—which can kill the small sea animals that pinnipeds feed on. Some pinnipeds are also threatened by pollution and hunting.

For thousands of years, humans have hunted pinnipeds for their blubber, fur, and meat. Some pinnipeds, such as Japanese sea lions, were hunted to **extinction**. Today, countries that allow seal hunts set limits on how many seals hunters can kill each year.

The Hawaiian monk seal is an **endangered** species.

Did You Know?

Seal hunting takes place in Canada, Greenland, Russia, Namibia, and Norway. The biggest hunt is in Canada. In 2008, more than 250,000 seals in Canada were killed by hunters.

A hunter captures a seal in the Arctic.

Hawaiian monk seals (only 1,200 left) and Mediterranean monk seals (just 400 left) are both highly endangered. Special laws now protect them from harm.

The Caribbean monk seal lived in the Caribbean Sea. The last ones were seen in 1952, near Jamaica. Despite many searches, none have been seen since, and in 1996 the species was declared extinct.

How Are Pinnipeds Used By Humans?

Seals, sea lions, and walruses can be seen in aquariums and zoos around the world. Sea lions are especially easy to train, and they remember what they learn. Some work as deep-sea divers for the U.S. military. Other sea lions are trained as "show animals" to jump through hoops and clap their flippers. But should these wild animals be used for entertainment or other human purposes?

Captive sea lions being used as show animals in a zoo

A sea lion attaches a line to a missile that was lost on the seabed.

Why does the U.S. military use sea lions?

In the United States, the Navy Marine Mammal Program trains sea lions to search for underwater objects such as mines (hidden bombs) and lost items. Sea lions can be better at this work than human divers. They can swim to the seabed more quickly than humans and can return to the surface faster. Video cameras are attached to the sea lions, and their progress is watched by their trainers onboard a ship.

 ### Did You Know?

A harbor seal called Hoover could imitate human speech. He lived at the New England Aquarium in Massachusetts in the 1970s. Hoover could make sounds that sounded like "Hello," "How are you?," and "Get out of here!"

Pinnipeds Around the World

Pinnipeds are found in every ocean and in many seas. Some species are found in just one place. For example, the Baikal seal lives only in Lake Baikal, Russia, and the Galápagos fur seal is found only on the Galápagos Islands.

Pacific walrus

The Pacific walrus is found in the North Pacific Ocean and in the Arctic region. It eats mainly shellfish, and a hungry adult can eat 6,000 clams in one meal!

Galápagos fur seal

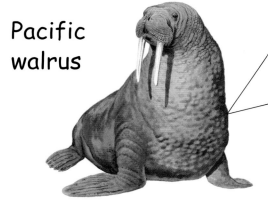

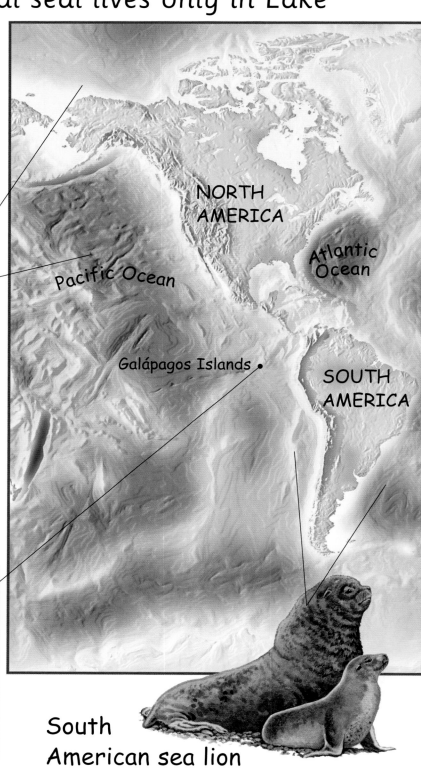

NORTH AMERICA

Pacific Ocean

Atlantic Ocean

Galápagos Islands

SOUTH AMERICA

South American sea lion

Baikal seal

Northern fur seal

The northern fur seal lives in the North Pacific Ocean, from the Bering Sea in the east to Japan in the west. It lives on fish and squid.

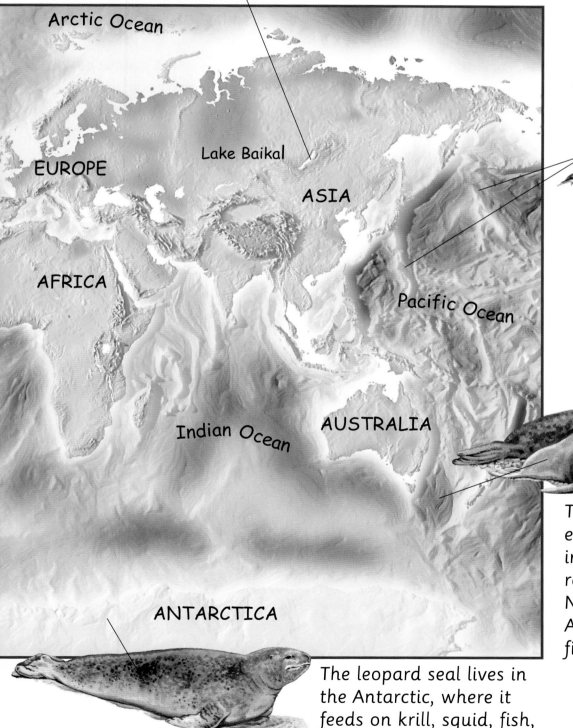

Arctic Ocean

EUROPE

AFRICA

Lake Baikal

ASIA

Pacific Ocean

Indian Ocean

AUSTRALIA

ANTARCTICA

Leopard seal

Southern elephant seal

The southern elephant seal lives in the Antarctic region, south of New Zealand and Australia. It eats fish and squid.

The leopard seal lives in the Antarctic, where it feeds on krill, squid, fish, and penguins.

Pinniped Facts

The average cruising speeds of some pinnipeds are:
- walrus: 5.6 mph (9 kph)
- sea lion: 10.6 mph (17 kph)
- fur seal: 18 mph (29 kph)

As much as half of a pinniped's body weight may be blubber.

An elephant seal has been found with 77 pounds (35 kg) of gastroliths in its stomach.

Inuit hunters in the Arctic listen for bearded seals under the ice. They put a kayak paddle in the water and put the handle end to their ear. The paddle picks up the sounds of the seals.

Some seals can sleep underwater. Elephant seals sometimes sleep deep underwater to save energy and to avoid predators. Others, such as the harbor seal, sleep with only their heads above the water. Male walruses sleep on the water's surface—they inflate their throat pouches to keep them afloat.

The average length of walrus tusks is about 14 inches (35 cm), but they can grow three times as long! These tusks never stop growing, but are worn down by the walrus chopping through ice.

Pinniped mothers have one baby at a time. The milk they feed to their babies contains up to 50 percent fat.

The Baikal seal is unusual because it spends all its life living in freshwater, not in salty seawater.

The sensitive whiskers on a pinniped's snout can detect movements nearby. In murky water, this is how pinnipeds find their prey. A walrus has about 700 whiskers.

Pinnipeds have been seen "playing" with fish. A California sea lion will catch a fish and then toss it into the air several times. When the sea lion loses interest, it swims away without bothering to eat the fish.

Unlike other marine mammals such as whales and dolphins, pinnipeds give birth on land and not in the sea.

Glossary

beaching When a whale becomes stranded on a shore.

blubber The thick layer of fat just under the skin of certain animals.

bull An adult male pinniped.

canine tooth A pointed tooth for tearing food.

carnivore An animal that eats other animals as its main food source.

colony A large group of animals of the same species that live together.

cow An adult female pinniped.

dialect A distinct set of sounds.

endangered At risk of dying out.

extinction The death of the last animal of a particular species.

gastroliths Stones in animals' stomachs that help to digest food.

global warming The gradual warming of Earth's atmosphere, caused in part by human activities.

haul-out A spot where pinnipeds come ashore.

krill Small, shrimp-like sea creatures.

lanugo Soft fur that covers some mammals before they are born.

mammal An animal that is born alive and then fed by its mother's milk.

migrate To travel between breeding and feeding places at certain times of the year.

molting Shedding old fur, skin, or hair. For pinnipeds, molting can be gradual (fur seals) or sudden (elephant seals).

odobenid (say: o-do-BEN-id) A kind of pinniped. The walrus is the only species in this family.

otariid (say: o-TAR-e-id) A kind of pinniped, also known as an eared seal. Otariids have ear flaps on the outside of their bodies.

phocid (say: FO-sid) A kind of pinniped, also known as a true seal or earless seal. Phocids have ear holes instead of flaps.

predator An animal that hunts other living creatures for food.

prey An animal that is hunted for food.

pup A young pinniped.

rookery A colony of breeding pinnipeds.

species A group of animals that look alike, behave in the same way, and can breed together.

weaned Able to eat solid food instead of mothers' milk.

Index